# Princess is Tired

## by Jay Dale
### illustrated by Mélanie Florian

a Capstone company — publishers for children

*Engage Literacy* is published in the UK by Raintree.
Raintree is an imprint of Capstone Global Library Limited, a company incorporated in England and Wales having its registered office at 264 Banbury Road, Oxford, OX2 7DY – Registered company number: 6695582

www.raintree.co.uk

Text copyright © UpLoad Publishing Pty Ltd 2021
Lead authors Jay Dale and Anne Giulieri

Editorial credits
Carrie Sheely, editor; Cynthia Della-Rovere, designer; Laura Manthe, production specialist

Illustrations copyright Capstone/Mélanie Florian

Printed and bound in China.

Princess is Tired
ISBN: 978 1 4747 9960 7

# Contents

## Chapter 1
# Princess stays up late

"Princess," said Mum, peeking round
the bedroom door.
"Please go to bed.
It's way too late to still be up."

"But Mum," replied Princess, "my new play
has to be finished by Thursday.
Today is Monday, and I have the trip
to the zoo tomorrow.
And Tuesday night is basketball practice
and Wednesday night is . . . "

5

"I know how busy you are," said Mum, before Princess could say any more. "And I know you love writing and basketball, and all the other amazing things you do. But it's important that you take care of yourself and get plenty of sleep."

"Please can I have just a little longer?" asked Princess. "Then I'll go to bed."

"Just 15 more minutes," replied Mum,
"but then off to sleep.
You have to be up early tomorrow.
The bus will be leaving at about 8 o'clock,
and I need to drive you to school first."

"I know, Mum," said Princess,
"but I'm nearly there!
My play is almost finished.
The kids are going to love it!"

Mum leaned down and gave Princess
a big hug.
"You know I'm super proud of you,"
she added.
"But even clever, funny and busy people
need sleep!"

## Chapter 2
# Too busy to sleep

Princess started to type a few words.
She suddenly felt very tired.
She looked at her alarm clock.
It said 9 o'clock.

"I really should go to bed," thought Princess.
But lots of other thoughts started to pop
into her head.
*What if she didn't get the play finished in time?*
*What if she missed the bus tomorrow morning?*
*What if she was so tired she forgot to take*
*her basketball to practice?*

Suddenly, Princess got really worried.
Lots and lots of thoughts were spinning
around inside her head.
She tried writing her play again but nothing
seemed to make any sense.

So she set her alarm for 7 o'clock
and got into bed.
But Princess was no longer sleepy.
She was wide awake with worry.
There was too much to do!
She tried closing her eyes.
That didn't work.

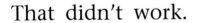

Then she tried closing her eyes and counting backwards from 100.

That didn't work.

Finally she turned on her bedside lamp and read for a while.

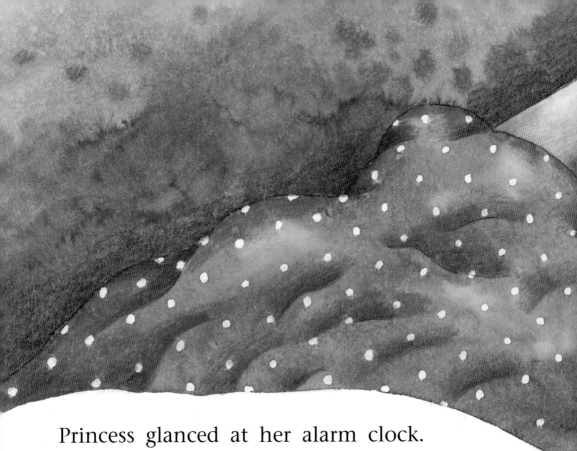

Princess glanced at her alarm clock.
It was 11 o'clock and she **still**
wasn't asleep.
She turned off her lamp and closed her eyes.
Then she did some slow breathing she had
been taught at school.
She breathed in and counted. 1, 2, 3, 4, 5, 6.
She breathed out and counted again.
1, 2, 3, 4, 5, 6.

The slow breathing really helped.
It slowed down her mind and stopped
all the busy thoughts in her head.

## Chapter 3

# A good lesson to learn

*Brrrring! Brrrring!*

Princess's alarm clock was ringing.

She had gone to sleep after all,

and now it was 7 o'clock in the morning.

"Good morning," said Mum.

"You have an exciting day ahead of you."

"Yes," said Princess sleepily.

"I have."

"Come on," said Mum.

"I'll help you get dressed.

You still have to eat breakfast before we go."

By the time Princess and Mum arrived
at school, Princess was feeling really tired.
Her head hurt, and she couldn't think clearly.
The other children were so excited
and very noisy.

"Good morning, Princess," said Mrs Kay.
"I hope you slept well.
It's going to be a big day today."

Princess just smiled.

On the way to the zoo, Princess was so tired she fell asleep on the bus.

"Hey, Princess," called Dara.
"Wake up!
We're at the zoo!"

As the excited children walked quickly
towards the gates of the zoo,
Princess was so tired that she couldn't
keep up with her friends.

The zoo was lots of fun.
Princess loved seeing her favourite animals,
the monkeys and the panda bears.
But she was still worried about all the work
she needed to do and how tired she felt.

"You don't seem yourself today, Princess,"
said Mrs Kay, as they all waited for the bus
to arrive.
"Are you okay?"

Princess gave Mrs Kay a tired smile.
"I didn't sleep very well last night," she said.
"I stayed up way too late."

"Ah!" said Mrs Kay.
"You need lots of sleep if you are going
to enjoy every day."

"Yes," said Princess.
"I've learned an important lesson today –
I need to get plenty of sleep.
Then I can always be at my best."

"That's a very good lesson to learn," smiled Mrs Kay.
"Even clever, funny and busy people like you, Princess, need sleep."

Princess smiled back.
"That's just what my mum says!"